DEDICATION
In Memoriam

Walter Irving Swanton

(1869 – 1943)

Lucy Ross Swanton

(1874 – 1933)

and

Sheldon Pettibone Clark

(1866 – 1930)

Hazel Baker Clark

(1883 – 1963)

Endorsements

Sheldon H. Clark's collection of poems *After the Fire A Still Small Voice* speaks to struggles of the human condition, loss and sorrow, the Fire which all of us encounter at some point in our lives. Each poem is a beautiful reflection on a verse from the Bible, offering fresh interpretations from Genesis to John. Sheldon shares words of encouragement and we hear the redemption, reconstruction, and resurrection of the "Still Small Voice." All is not lost, there is always hope. The minimalism of each poem serves only to deepen the impact upon the reader, as each word brims with significance. In sharing these thought-provoking poems, Sheldon gives us the opportunity for contemplation and new insight into the Bible verses and our own emotions. *After the Fire a Still Small Voice* speaks to the soul.

Siân Bowen-Cole, B.A. (Hons) Coventry Polytechnic, U.K.
P.G.C.E. Portsmouth Polytechnic, U.K.
A PGCE is a Post Graduate Certificate in Education

Sheldon Clark's poems spoke to me immediately. I had no preconceptions as to what to expect. As an artist, my process was to read each poem, allow the descriptive writing to form mental impressions for potential lines, shapes and visual atmosphere. Specifically, I chose charcoal because it is an ancient medium direct from the fire and has a glow-like quality without equal. I used raw sienna and black. Sienna provokes feelings of safety and warmth, like a welcome embrace, while black suggests a colder distant reality, perhaps even a harshness, which evokes the need for the "listener" to be alert, aware, and present. I enjoyed Clark's minimalist approach in his poetry as they inspired me to react, engage, and then to depict what I was sensing.

Catherine Farquhar, AOCAD
Ontario College of Art and Design

Complementary to the verbal is the visual. Each poem expresses a word-image. Each picture speaks to the imagination. Both forms of expression support each other in an existential dance. Sheldon's deeply moving poetry is the embodiment of devotion and human kindness. Catherine's dreamy renderings serve as a touchstone to Sheldon's words. Thank you both for sharing your art.

George S. Keltika, B.F.A., B.Ed.
University of Windsor

Foreword

The minimalist approach in **After the Fire A Still Small Voice**, heeds the pseudo-proverb, *"One picture is worth a thousand words,"* and the advice, attributed to St. Francis of Assisi, *"Preach the Gospel. If necessary, use words."*

Selected quotations are from the authorized **King James Bible**. The challenge was for the author to write, and then for the artist to sketch their respective inspirations. The pattern was to select a quotation, compose a meditation, and then ask the artist to create a drawing to add still other voices to the ancient, and yet, contemporary story of human encounter with the divine from beginnings to future hope. The creative interface between the poems and the abstract-expressionist charcoal drawings are devised to complement each other.

The astute reader will discern thematic development from ancient Hebrew texts to C.E. accounts of causation, dynamic settings, particularities of time and place, emotional struggle, maturation, and insight hidden in the paradoxical shadow world of the perennial divine mystery. Light and dark are juxtaposed to produce dynamic tension. What is implied is as important as what is explicit. Imaginative projection, connotative values, and non-traditional creative interpretation are keys to expanded transformative understanding.

The observant art aficionado will see in the Abstract Expressionist charcoal sketches little of representative reality. Instead, the artist created from swirls, dark specks (voices?), vertical horizontal circular energy, emotive forces, light source, silhouetted figures, womb-like contours, explosions of presence and absence, intensity, the chalice viewed Daliesque from above, disregard for convention, and tendered security in the eternal sway between the earth-bound and the transcendental.

Sheldon H. Clark, D. Min.

Acknowledgements

Influences who inspired *After the Fire A Still Small Voice* are gratefully acknowledged. They include: Sian Bowen-Cole, the late Sheldon P. Clark, 1866–1930 (Artist), Hazel B. Clark, 1883–1963, Catherine Farquhar (Artist), Edna and Alasdair Farquhar, Sofia Grimaldi (technical), Mary Hutchings, George Keltika (Artist), the late Fr. Tom McKillop, 1928–2012 (Priest and Poet), Amber McPhail, Foxlo McPhail, Ryan McPhail (Artist), the late Neil Paul, 1940–2021 (Teacher, Poet), the late John Punshon, 1935–2017 (Quaker, Teacher, Author), Christine Richardson (Ballet Dancer and Teacher, Fellow and Examiner CC-CICB), David Richardson, LVO (Writer, Artist, friend and *'saunterer through the floating world'*), David Stover (Editor and Publisher, Rock's Mills Press), and the late Gilbert Stafford, Ph.D. (1938–2008), Dean of Anderson University School of Theology.

Sheldon H. Clark, D. Min.

Previous Publications

Poetry and Prayer Sketches, by Sheldon H. Clark, artwork by George Keltika, 2013, 2020
Voices Extended, by Neil Paul and Sheldon H. Clark, graphics by Ed VandenDool, 2016
Still Voices, by Sheldon H. Clark, graphics by Ed VandenDool, 2020, 2021

After the Fire A Still Small Voice is published by
Rock's Mills Press
www.rocksmillspress.com
For information, please contact us at customer.service@rocksmillspress.com.

Copyright © 2022 by Sheldon H. Clark (words)
Copyright © 2022 by Catherine Farquhar (artwork)
All rights reserved. Reproduction in whole or in part without the express written permission of the copyright holder is prohibited.

For Understanding

He that readeth these things, let him not strive to comprehend them; but be content with what he feeleth thereof suitable to his own present estate, and as the life grows in him, and he in the life ... the words ... will of themselves open to him.

Isaac Penington (1617 – 1679)
Quaker Mystic

CREATION

*Out of dark's division,
light emerges fragile each day,
while sea anemones and wildflowers materialize,
waving beautifully as the slush and swirl
of undercurrents, shifting tides,
and air whiffs power undertows,
moon tides, mountain slides, prairie twirls,
contest renewed darkness*

KNOWLEDGE

*God saw the light, that it was good: and
God divided the light from the darkness.
Genesis 1: 4*

AFTER THE FIRE

*Tumultuous landscape churned destruction
from what was into nada-scape,
a smoked canvas after the fire,
away from cries and frenzied death,
into the centering calm,
a still small voice.*

A STILL SMALL VOICE

*And after the earthquake a fire; but the Lord was
not in the fire: and after the fire a still small voice.
I Kings 19: 12*

DUST AND ASHES

*Scarlet and golden plumage flumes
cascade into the consuming flames
repeating the timeless process of
regeneration, acknowledging
hope and love, from which
destructive devastation
will emerge aspirations,
imaginings, dreams.
visions.*

*Repent in dust and ashes ...
And the Lord restored the fortunes of Job
when he prayed for his friends ...
Job 42:6b, 10a (NRSV)*

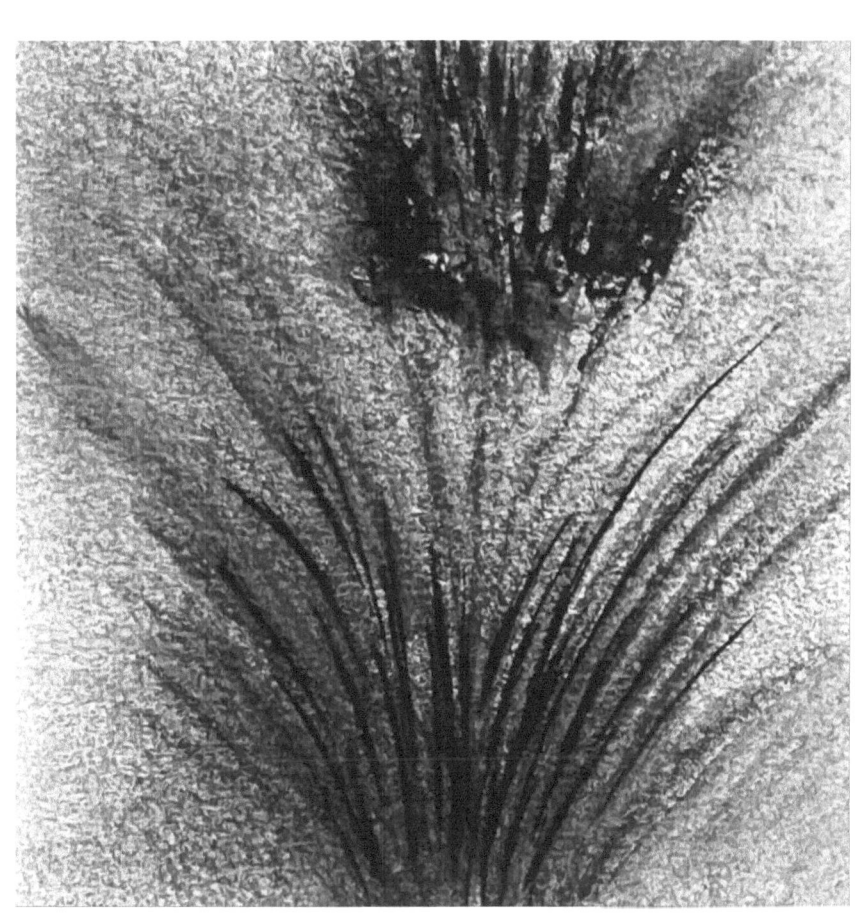

A POTTER'S VESSEL

*Strewn haphazardly
trampled shards from the greater
vessel they once inhabited
was a seamless utilitarian
entity that waited patiently
for reconstruction, and once
unearthed, rendered reassembled
afresh from a jigsaw puzzle
amplifying perseverance
and love.*

*Serve the Lord with fear, and rejoice with trembling.
Blest are all they that put their trust in him.
Psalm 2: 9b, 11,12b*

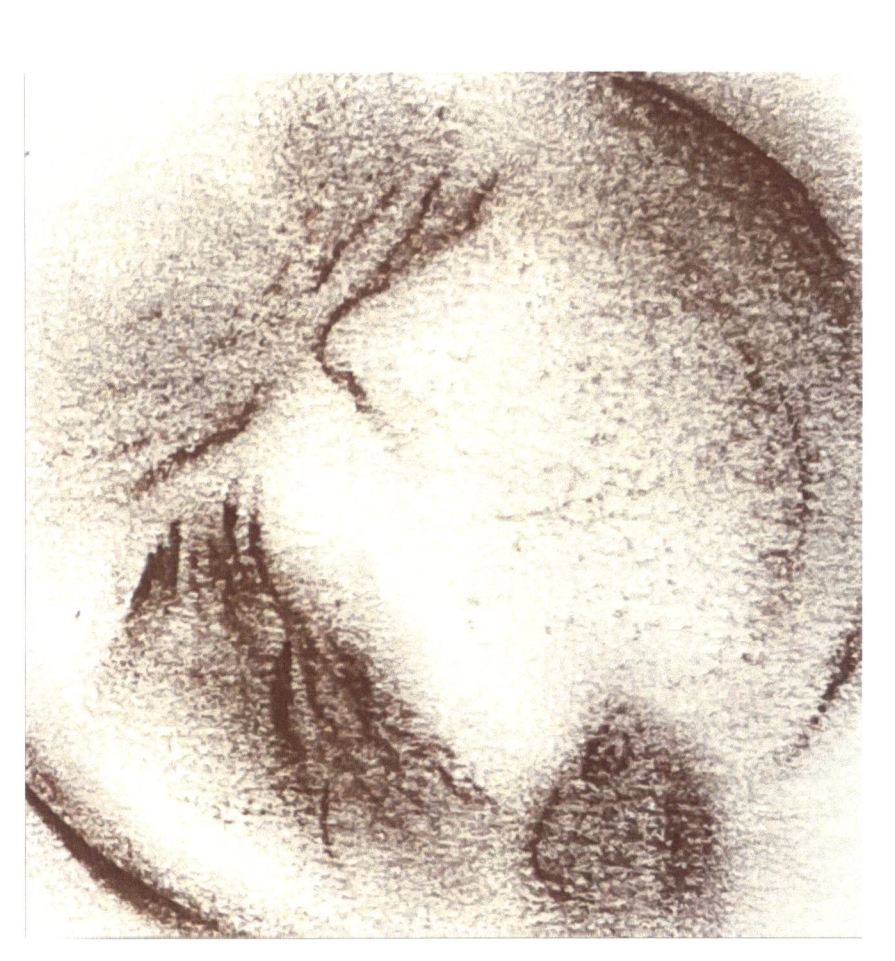

PEACE

**The Spirit knows no weaponry
only the abiding omnipresence of compassion
lifted beyond mere physical constructs,
which explode to smithereens
temporal structures of finite consequence
into the infinite heaven of
Divine Love.**

*He maketh wars to cease unto the end of the earth;
he breaketh the bow, and cutteth the spear in sunder;
he burneth the chariot of fire. Be still and know that I am God.
Psalm 46:9-10a*

THE HILLS

*Awakened morning cast glimmers
flickering toward retreating darkness,
shaping shadows into visible forms
beholding nature's blushed contours,
and human preoccupations merging,
inspiring ideals, adventures,
repentance, loveliness,
to approach that which is
Divine.*

*I will lift up my eyes unto the hills, from whence cometh my help.
My help cometh from the Lord, which made heaven and earth.
Psalm 121: 1, 2*

EMPATHY

*Come and sit quietly with open
head, heart, hands,
discover inner health
as though for the first time
like the source from a mountain spring,
a friendly greeting from an old friend,
an insight into visionary expectations,
and drink from the Cup
from which
I drink.*

Can ye drink of the cup that I drink of?
Mark 10:39

WISDOM

**Death in drying tears gives hope
for new love, not a sentimental replacement
one for one, but expressions caring
beyond grief, gratitude for what once was,
release to future adventures,
recognition that Love is
the most potent force.**

*Therefore, all things whatsoever ye would that men should do to you,
do ye even so to them: for this is the law and the prophets.
Matthew 5: 12*

TRANSFORMATION

**We encounter a spiritual bond,
which transports our souls to
mystical shoals questing anointment,
so that the other may be, become, and
fulfill their created purpose and
receive Divine blessings.**

*Henceforth I call you not servants;
but I have called you friends.
John 15:15*

FLAMES OF FIRE

**Campfires tell stories of survival,
la chasse, the sacred, mythic encounters,
folk tales, friendly and terrifying ghosts,
humor, memories, exploits, successes,
star-filled heavens, fantasy, feats, traditions;
we listen to dancing flames
leaping from embers to Truth.**

UNDERSTANDING

*And there appeared unto them cloven tongues, and it sat
upon each of them. And they were filled with the Holy ghost, and …
the Spirit gave them utterance.
Acts 2: 3, 4*

COUNSEL

**Listen to the falling rain
singing cleanliness to dusty thoughts
when children played 'dress-up' in attics,
looked through forgotten stereopticons
to rainbow worlds, rocked a cradled doll,
and let their imaginations
conceive friendship, devotion,
abiding joy, peace.**

GOODNESS

*The fruit of the Spirit is love, joy, peace, longsuffering, gentleness,
goodness, faith, meekness, temperance: against such there is no law.
Galatians 5: 22, 23*

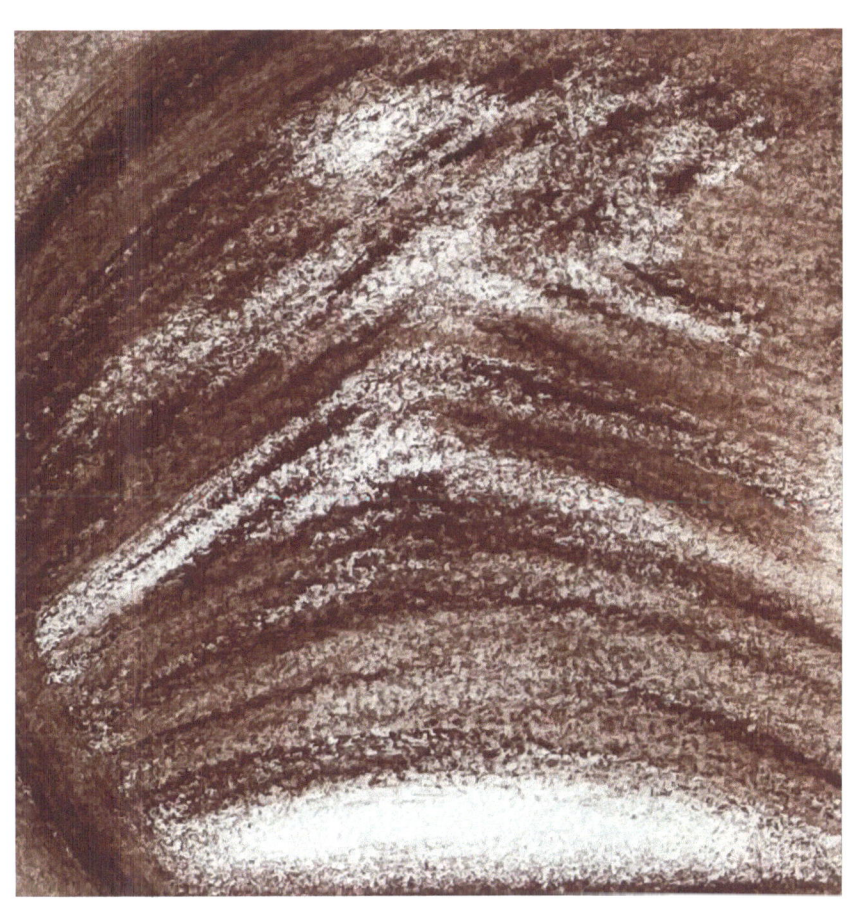

FORTITUDE

Narcissistic self-hatred, suicidal philandering, wounded worried drunkard, spiritually maimed being, was led to health by combinations of medical intervention, and persistent consistent therapies of truthfulness, forgiveness, acceptance, unconditional love.

HONESTY

Let your communication be, Yea, yea; Nay, nay.
Matthew 5:37

PIETY

*Playing hide-and-seek
with eye-crossed fingers let vision
see another dimension to private prayer,
soundless petitions, thanksgivings,
mercy, grief, guidance, aspirations,
eons away from public view,
silent reverent intonements,
held in the Light.*

*When thou prayest, enter into thy closet, and when thou
hast shut the door, pray to thy Father which is in secret.
Matthew 6: 6*

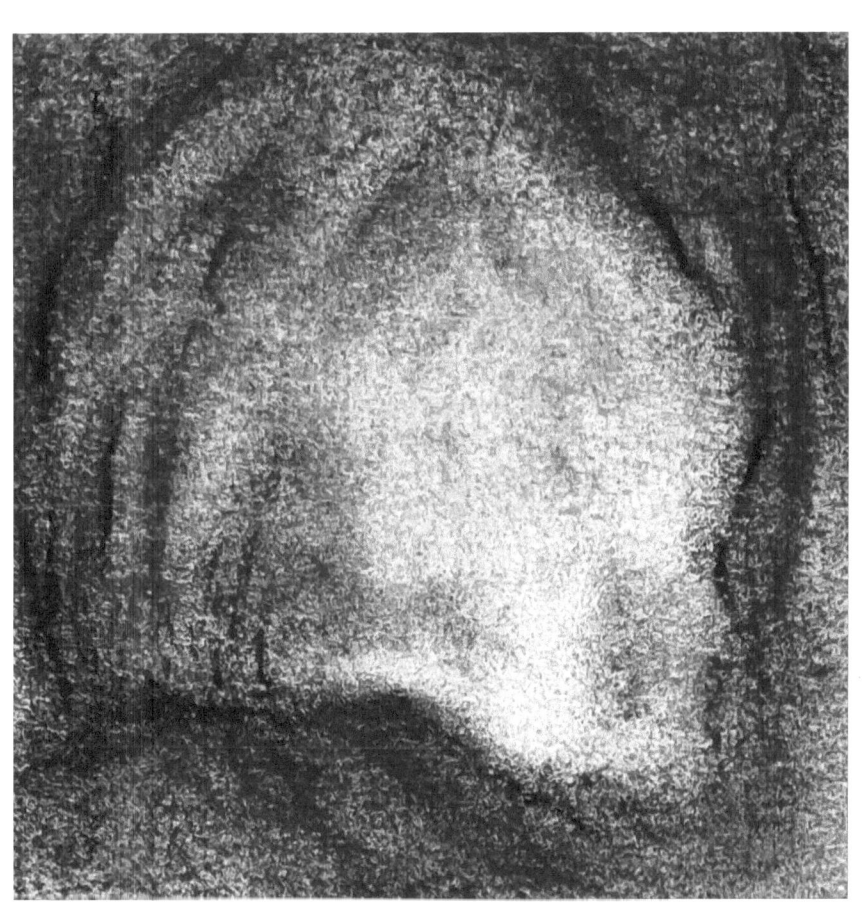

COMMUNION

**After the fire a still small voice
wordless, just a breath, the divine mystery
enshrined in an act, the offering, a pursed sip
from the vessel, understood by friend and foe alike,
acceptance, forgiveness, blessing, peace,
secure Eternal Love.**

Jesus took the bread, and blessed it, and brake it, and gave it to the disciples, and said, Take, eat; this is my body. And he took the cup, and gave thanks, and gave it to them, saying, Drink ye all of it: for this is my blood for the new testament.
Matthew 26: 26-28; Mark 14: 22-24; Luke 22: 17-20

SERVANT-LEADERSHIP

*Enabling the other to shine
equipping recognition, identifying
spiritual generosity, linking one to the other,
especially forgiveness diminished nothing,
confirmed, even uplifted common achievement
to the apex of appreciative thankfulness.*

He riseth from supper, and laid aside his garments; and took a towel, and girded himself. After that he poureth water into a bason, and began to wash the disciples' feet, and to wipe them with the towel.
John 13: 4, 5

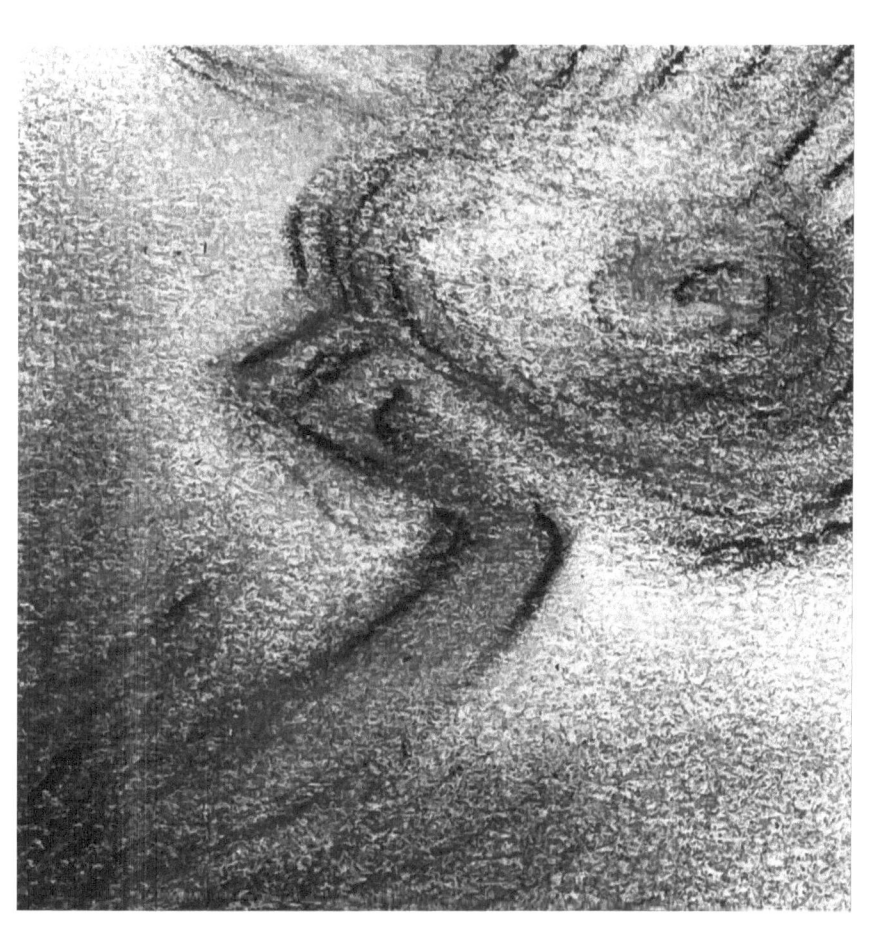

DEATH

*Inevitable, often predictable,
and then, the opaque happening
as no words describe the ultimate divide,
"alive, breath, crossed," that great mystery
of being and not-being, the line intangible,
unable to be grasped and The Light
shines in all its Glory.*

*And they bring him unto the place Golgotha, which is,
being interpreted, The place of the skull . . .
And Jesus cried with a loud voice, and gave up the ghost.
Mark 15:22, 37*

EMMAUS

*A figure, a voice, a chance encounter
on the way, strangers chattered
current events of a tale of betrayal,
trial, execution, as though prophetic:
once arrived He took, blessed,
broke, gave the bread;
the crossing validated, we witnessed
His ascension with Truth and Grace
into Divine Love.*

*And they said to one another, did not our heart burn within us,
while he talked with us by the way, and while he opened to us the scriptures?
Luke 24: 32*

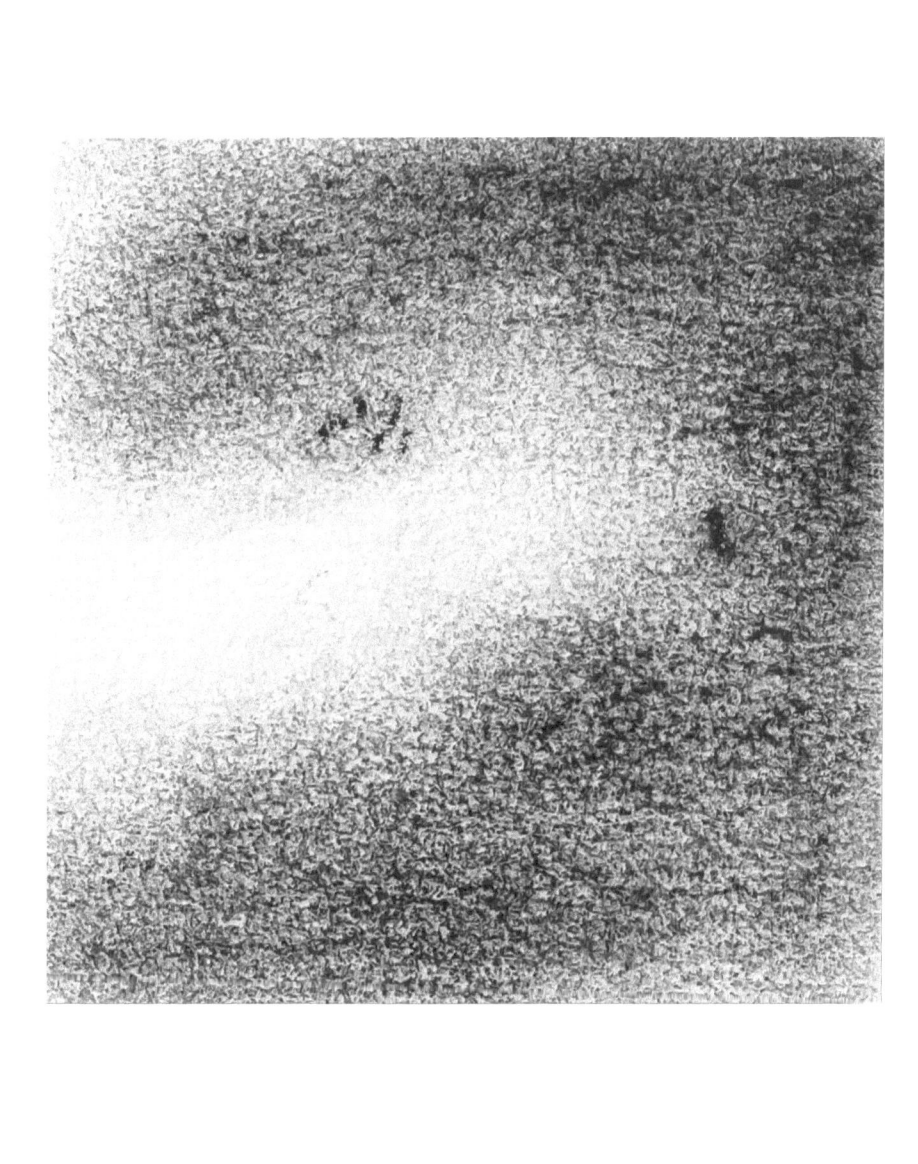

SANCTUARY

**The black and white pair circled,
herded, lay down, watched, attentive;
one focused, circled the near course;
the other, alert, waited, focused,
crouched along the far arc,
the Good Shepherd's crook pointed,
silently they found the
Gate to the Fold.**

*Jesus saith unto Simon Peter, Simon, son of Jonas, lovest thou me more than these?
He saith unto him, Yea, Lord; thou knowest that I love thee. He saith unto him . . .
Feed my lambs . . . Feed my sheep . . . Feed my Sheep . . . Follow me.
John 21: 15, 16, 17, 19*

www.ingramcontent.com/pod-product-compliance
Lightning Source LLC
Chambersburg PA
CBHW050747110526
44590CB00003B/100